Moses and the Exodus Express

Paul Kerensa

Illustrated by Liz and Kate Pope

spck

A long time ago, lived a King SO bad,
He wanted rid of the boys – even this young lad.

So the **baby** was hidden . . .
Mum **hushed** with a '**Shoosh!**',
Put his **basket** on the **river**
and **pushed**, with a *whoosh!*

The **baby** on board sailed along, round the bend,

Till he landed **on shore** – his trip at an end.

The King's helpful daughter
was doing her washing,
And found the young baby
a-splishing and a-sploshing.

Though her father was **nasty**, the princess was **kinder**,

So she asked the boy's mum,

'Would you be his childminder?

He will play, nice and safe, under both of our noses.

And his name, well, who knows . . .

I suppose, could be Moses?'

Moses grew up, seeing family and friends

Made slaves by the King, for his own wicked ends.

They were stuck in a rut, at the end of the line,

No train out of town and no exit sign.

Moses was filled with sadness and doubt,

They needed a leader, to find a way out.

'That leader's not me,' Moses thought, as he walked.

'Yes it is!' said a **bush** . . .

that caught **fire** as it **talked!**

Here's a **public announcement**
from **God** for the **nation**:
'That **building** they're building . . .
let's make it a station!
Tell the King that you're leaving,
for a **new home address.**
One-way tickets for all –
on my **Exodus Express!**'

visitor information

But when Moses demanded, the King gave a *sneer*:

'I regret that my slaves' travel terminates here.

I ***can't*** let them go! They ***need*** to work harder!

So planned engineering works stop their departure.'

Moses said, 'God won't accept your delays,

So shortly arriving, on platform ten: *plagues*!

They'll bring to your palace: darkness and lice,

And famine and flies . . . until you think twice.'

The skies became **dark** and the river turned **red**,

Till the King tapped his loudspeaker,

sighed and then said:

'I'd like to apologize for the delay,

Your late-running service

may get under way.'

The people rejoiced and they chugged out of town,

But the King changed his mind,

so he signalled, 'Slow down!'

Too late! Moses led all his people as planned:

The non-stop express for the

new Promised Land.

But the **half-million** people
soon **stopped** in their tracks,
In front of them **SEA**,
and the King at their backs.

Moses just **trusted**
that God knew the way,
So he looked at the water –
and started to **pray**.

The sea began swirling,

waves crashing and tossing,

The water revealed a new channel crossing!

So the journey continued, the people moved *faster* . . .

The King's men behind them

were nearing disaster.

Moses and passengers tried not to *slip*

As they raced **underwater**

to finish their trip.

They clambered and climbed
over stones, rocks and boulders,
while seawater fell on the King and his soldiers.

The sea settled back to the calmest of waters,

The King had an early bath, with his supporters.

God's plan had conquered;
the King's had backfired –
His journey diverted,
his ticket expired.

For Moses and friends,

this was just one more station:

The far Promised Land

was their end destination.

So next time it seems that

you're stuck – no way back –

Keep on trusting in God

and he'll keep you on track.

First published in Great Britain in 2018

Society for Promoting Christian Knowledge
36 Causton Street, London SW1P 4ST
www.spck.org.uk

British Library Cataloguing-in-Publication Data
A catalogue record for this book is avaliable from the British Library

ISBN 978–0–281–07757–1

1 3 5 7 9 10 8 6 4 2

Typeset and designed by Anna Lubecka, Banana Bear Books

Printed in Turkey by Imago

Produced on paper from sustainable forests